To...

From...

Purple Ronnie's Bloke's Guide to Life, The Universe and Bottom Burps

poo-ee

by Purple Ronnie

First published 2008 by Boxtree
an imprint of Pan Macmillan Ltd
Pan Macmillan, 20 New Wharf Road, London N1 9RR
Basingstoke and Oxford
Associated companies throughout the world
www.panmacmillan.com

ISBN 978-0-7522-2685-9

The material in this book was previously published under the titles
Purple Ronnie's Guide to Life, Purple Ronnie's Guide to Men, Purple Ronnie's Guide to Girls,
Purple Ronnie's Book of Love and The Smashing World of Purple Ronnie

'Purple Ronnie' created by Giles Andreae. The right of Giles Andreae and Janet Cronin
to be identified respectively as the author and illustrator of this work has been asserted by them
in accordance with the Copyright, Designs and Patents Act 1988.

1 3 5 7 9 8 6 4 2

A CIP catalogue record for this book is available from
the British Library.

Printed and bound in Italy by L.E.G.O. SpA

Visit www.panmacmillan.com to read more about all our books
and to buy them. You will also find features, author interviews and
news of any author events, and you can sign up for e-newsletters
so that you're always first to hear about our new releases.

THIS BOOK IS DEDICATED
TO ALL MY FRIENDS
AROUND THE WORLD

The Beginning of Time

Imagine a place where there were no burgers or beer or hot dogs

Imagine a place without chips or chocolate or chocolate chips or ketchup or anything

Imagine a place where there's nothing to natter about and no-one to cuddle up with

Imagine a place where nothing's ever on T.V. and there's no T.V. not to watch it on

Imagine a place where it's night all the time, where it's cold and dark and lonely

That's what it was like in the beginning of time when the only person around was GOD

Not surprisingly God didn't think it was much fun.
He was bored and lonely and sometimes quite scared

And because it was dark he quite
often bumped into things

When God went to bed he used to shut his eyes
and dream for hours about inventing this place that
he could muck around and have fun in

There would be all sorts of smells and feelings and tastes in this place and every day there would be friends to explore new things with

He wanted something like a gigantic bouncy castle with flowers and trees and monkeys and butterflies and streams and mountains and stuff like that

Then all of a sudden God had a brilliant idea. He saved up loads of his most powerful magic and mixed it up with his biggest wishes then he sprinkled on top his most powerful spell in history

EVER

That night God didn't have any dreams at all and when he looked out of the window the next day he felt smashing

Dangling from the roof of the sky was a sort of gigantic round pudding

All the grooviest treats and surprises he'd ever wanted were stuffed inside that pudding. what's more he was the king of it

yippee!

swing

HO HO HO

For the first time in his life God laughed...

...He had invented THE WORLD

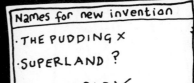

Names for new invention
• THE PUDDING ✗
• SUPERLAND ?
• THE WORLD ✓
• NORMAN SNACKELFIZZER ✗
  ↑ too muddly

?

What is Life?

Everything that moves has a life inside it and the Life is the bit that makes them work.

The Life inside a tree is very lazy so it just hangs around and grows but the Life inside an animal just can't stop wriggling and jumping around

gambol   skip   Jitter   Jive   ?

Life is the bit that makes...

Bebopalula she's my baby

CRISPS

Flowers want to open... Whales want to sing... and people want to watch T.V.

There is a Life inside every person and even though there are zillions of them each Life makes its owner completely different from everyone else

Life can make you so happy you just want to burst out of your skin with it or so sad you just want to curl up and sink into the ground

This whole book is about all the different bits of Life. It goes from before it STARTS to what happens when it GOES AWAY and there's lots of IN-BETWEEN bits as well.

Life

Life is a sort of a person machine
That fits in a hole in your tummy
And privately tickles your laughing device
When somebody says something funny

Life is the bit that goes droopy and flat
Whenever you're lonely or sad
And somersaults round in the top of your head
When you're in love or just glad

Most of the time it just jiggles around
But when you're asleep in your bed
It goes on adventures in dangerous lands
And feeds them back into your head

Once when it thought I was sleeping
I secretly opened my eyes
And just caught a glimpse of it climbing back in
With cowboys and pirates and spies

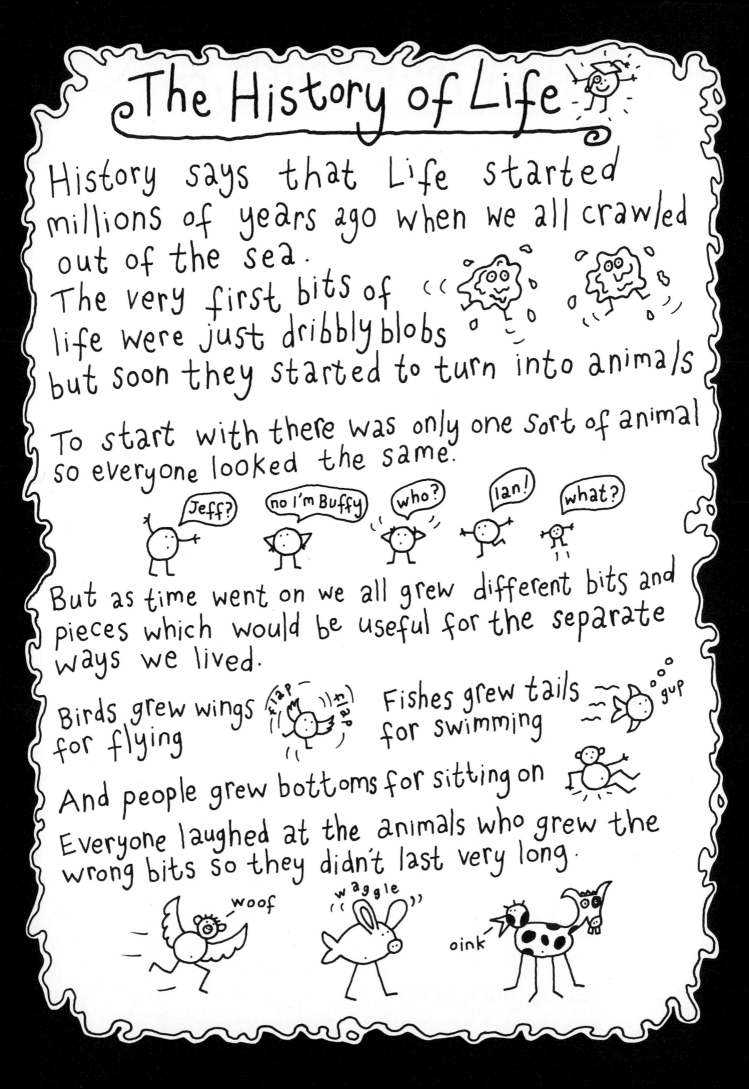

The First People

The first people were Adam and Eve. They lived in the world when it was almost brand new. The trouble is they couldn't find any instructions to go with it

Because of this they quite often got in a muddle about how to work all the new things and what it was like to be people

First of all they went around completely bare

When they felt hungry they didn't know what to eat or how to get it into their tummies

And when they felt saucy they had to try
millions of experiments before they got it right

Adam and Eve thought that
Doing It was one of the
best inventions ever, so they
had millions of babies who
all found girlfriends or
boyfriends and had
millions more babies

In the end all the different places in the world
became full of people. Most of them were friendly and
polite but some of them are still very naughty

Because of this God had to make a list of important
instructions which people must <u>never</u> forget

These are the main ones...

INSTRUCTIONS FOR LIVING

1. Thou shalt not have rude thoughts about thy mate's girlfriend

2. Thou art not allowed Ketchup _and_ mustard with thy sausages

3. Thou shalt not leave hairy bits in the bath

4. If thy enemy bashes thee in thou shalt ask him to bog off politely

5. Thou shalt always say thy girlfriend looks fantastic when she dresses up

6. Thou shalt not point at baldies

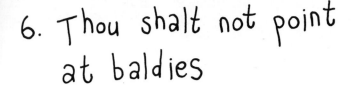

7. If thou eatest not thy meat thou canst not have any pudding

8. Thou shalt not waft thy bottom burps towards other people and pretend that thou was not the maker of the bottom burp in the first place

9. Thou shalt not try to escape the washing up

10. Thou shalt not squash thy girlfriend out of the bed, nor shalt thou hog the blankets

IF YOU DO NOT OBEY THESE INSTRUCTIONS YOU GO STRAIGHT TO HELL ⇨

How to Make a Life

First of all the Mum and Dad get together in a secret place in the middle of the night

They cuddle and Kiss for ages and say all sorts of soppy things to eachother

Then they put on their electric pants and when they plug them in there's a huge explosion and the Life just flies into the Mum

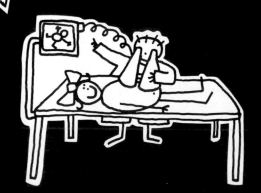

At first the Life is so tiny that you can only see it with a ginormous pair of binoculars

But if the Mum eats loads of grub and sings to it then it grows

The Mum then goes into hospital and the doctor attaches her to a machine which makes sure the Life has all the right bits

giblets ✓
brains ✓
tummy button ✓
toe nails ✓

At last when everyone is ready the Mum does the baby in her bed

OUR SCHOOL OUTING

One day the teacher said she would take our class to a museum and she asked us which one we would like to go to

explosions and killing

skeletons and people's insides

slugs and worms

But the girls won although their idea was by far the worst

please Miss could we go to a place that has pretty paintings and interesting things from history

yes shirlee what a good idea

First of all Teacher showed us some really boring pictures and she didn't even let us have ice-creams

Bored Girlie

This painting was done by a dead person from Italy

SOPPY SUNSET

Flick

oh isn't it romantic

Then we had to look at masses of pictures of flowers and people in the Bible and stuff

After that we went to the room of messy blobs and scribbles by trendy and modern people

Then we found the expert who showed us a room that the teacher said was closed

and the nice man explained something to us

When we got back to school Teacher asked us if we'd had a nice day

She said one day our paintings might be in a museum

This is a

Lazy Poem

I hate getting up in the morning
And doing my work every day
I'd rather stay in and watch telly
Or eat loads of chocolates and play

by Purple Ronnie

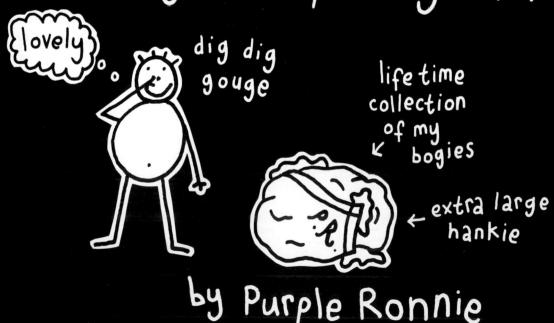

a poem about
↓
SPOTS

a splatted spot →

There's nothing wrong with having spots
In fact it's a wonderful feeling
When you line up a ripe one
Concentrate hard
And squeeze till it splats

← a ripe one

on the ceiling

by Purple Ronnie

a poem saying
↓
I Like You

You tell me I'm fat and I'm ugly
You tell me I'm utterly nuts
You tell me I burp and I fart
and I smell
But that's why I like you so
much

by Purple Ronnie

Friends

One of the things that makes life great is friends

my mates ←

shirlee Gordon me Maisy Nev

Even being very sexy and rich is useless if you haven't got friends

Norman No-mates

I'm so lonesome

speed

vroom

FLASH 1

bounce

Because friends are what make things FUN

If you're feeling sad friends can take away your sadness

And if you're feeling happy friends can double the happiness

Friends can make all sorts of things worth doing that you would never do on your own

And friends can make everyday things feel like you're doing them for the first time

Friends can be nosey and friends can get you into trouble

But REAL FRIENDS are the smashingest things you can have

a poem about ↓

Friends

Some people think that it's great
to be rich
To be cool and keep up with the
trends
But riches and looks just don't
matter at all
Cos what really counts is your
friends

no cash →

Nev's latest tie ←

Smashing mates →

by Purple Ronnie

a poem for an

Extra Special Friend

If I had a million pounds
I know what I would do
I'd buy some extra special times
And spend them all with you

by Purple Ronnie

a poem about a smelly person ↓

Smelly

pong whiff

You take off your shirt
And your armpits are whiffy
You take off your socks
And your feet are all niffy
You give me a hug
And you're terribly smelly
Then you ask me to kiss you
-NOT ON YOUR NELLIE

by Purple Ronnie

Bottom Burping

Bottom burps are one of the most useful and amazing things you can do

Sometimes they go off completely by mistake and at other times you can load them up in your bottom bit by bit and fire them out at precisely the right moment

Some of the best uses for bottom burps are:

making room in crowded spaces

embarrassing other people

& showing off to friends at Bottom Matches

Boys & Girls

At first boys think girls are rubbish but when they get older they start to think of them in a different way

As soon as boys begin to dream about hugging and kissing girls all the time horrid things happen to them

Their voices
go all wobbly →

Hair grows out
of their faces →

Their voices go all wobbly, hair grows

They smell and get
covered in spots →

But girls just get prettier and prettier

This means that boys have to learn tricks to make girls fancy them. Here are some of the best ones

↓

1. When you talk to girls, don't say too much about how amazing you are but tell them all sorts of things about themselves

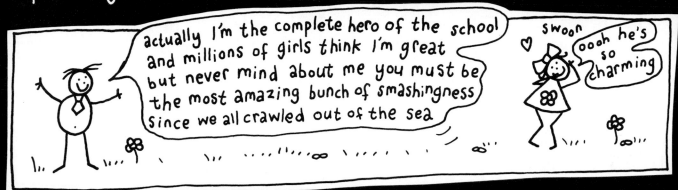

2. A very good trick is always to tell pretty girls you think they're brainy and tell brainy girls you think they're pretty

3. Always be as mysterious as possible

4. When you're with a girl, don't keep telling your mates how you think it's going

5. Don't show off about eating and drinking and making horrid smells. Girls don't like that kind of showing off

6. Quite a good way to make a girl fancy you is to pretend you fancy someone else

what is a Grown-up ?

Grown-ups can be young or old or anywhere in the middle. What makes you a Grown-up is not how long you have been alive but how **IMPORTANT** and **SERIOUS** your brain feels. Here is a guide on how to spot them:

Grown-ups listen to music that doesn't have any words

Grown-ups learn long words so that people will think they are very important

Grown-ups are useless at making up games so they just stand around and say things

Grown-ups think business and newspapers are the most interesting things in the world

The Great Big Grown-up Hunt

When I went to Grown-up Land
I wore my best disguise
And Neville made a Grown-up hunting thing
Cos if you want to study them
It must be a surprise
And that's the sort of stuff you need to bring

~

They never like to skip and dance
Or muck around and play
They've always got their grown-up things to do
Like officing their businesses
And shopping things all day
And reading grown-up papers in the loo

~

They've even got a funny way
of doing up their hair
The ladies paint theirs blue or pink or red
The gentlemen just lose it all
But make-believe it's there
By scraping little bits across their head

~

We tracked some to their bedroom
Where we got a big surprise
Cos both of them had taken off their kit
The gentleman was gurgling
And rolling round his eyes
But the lady didn't seem to mind a bit

He frolicked and he wriggled
And he bounced with all his might
But Neville said we shouldn't make a fuss
Cos interrupting Lady-Bouncing
Might not be polite
And we didn't want him bouncing round on us

When we'd done our studying
My friends all gathered round
And after thinking very hard I said
"Grown-ups are the curiousest
animals I've found
I think I'd rather be a ME instead"

by Purple
Ronnie

a poem about
↓
Bottom Burps

PFFRT

^ a bottom burp

If your **BOTTOM** burps in
                    public
Try to say in time
"Goodness gracious what
                    a whiff
It doesn't smell like mine"

me running for it
-having just
done one

PFFRT

Poo-eee   Poo-eee

by purple Ronnie

a poem about
↓
Bottie Coughs

Why do people's Bottie Coughs
Smell of eggs and ham?
I wish they smelt of apple pie
Or scrumptious strawberry jam

eggy
whiff
FFRRP
pooee
JAM 'O' FRESH

by Purple Ronnie

SWEARING

Swearing is great but it can be difficult to do properly unless you have had a lot of practice

Safety

First of all you must learn the rules because swearing can be very dangerous indeed

The Rules of Swearing

1. DO NOT swear at things that are bigger than you

2. NEVER swear in tight spaces

3. ALWAYS have a getaway route planned

4. NEVER swear at friends - even if you're only joking

Choosing Your Words

For the best swears you must choose your words very carefully. You often only get one good chance for each swear so you must not fluff it

um blimey...er it... um whiffle

help Purp

?

fancy a snog?

← swear dictionary

Word Groups

Here are some of the best words arranged into groups

Surprise Words		Bottom Words		Noise Words
crikey	*	Botty	!	Crackle
Heck		Pants		whiff
Flip	◎	Willy	☆	Fizz
Blimey		Fart		Pop

Pick a word from each group to help make great swears. Practise with small swears first and slowly make them longer. You can even add some of your own words

☆ You **must** use the word "off" if you want to do an angry or rude swear ☆

Here is a Happy swear

hey purple you've just won 20p

Hooray How flipping botty smashing

POOLS

. . .

Here is an unhappy swear

hey purple you're chucked

oh hecking whiffy Panthead

If you get it right a good swear can feel smashing.
Here are some examples of where it is useful :

Getting Rid of Pests

Showing off to Friends

Frightening Old People

HAPPY SWEARING

a shy poem
↓
To Someone I Like

I sometimes find it rather
                              hard

To say I really care

And that I like you quite
                              a lot

But I've said it now -
                          so there

hot flush

by Purple
   Ronnie

a poem about

Missing You

There are times when I really
do miss you
And think of you missing me too
So I close my eyes tight
And I daydream
That I am together with you

lovely daydream

by Purple
Ronnie

a recipe for Love Pie

by Purple Ronay

Take a pint of tickle juice
And whisk it till it's thick
Pick a crop of cuddle fruit
And crush them with a stick

♥

Nibble eighteen earlobes
As gently as you can
Then grate a little botty kiss
And put it in the pan

♥

Dip a snog in snuggle sauce
And let it rest a while
Then soak it in hug marinade
and season with a smile

♥

Add a pinch of happy spice
Grown in huggle town
And bake it in the oven
Till it comes out
golden brown

Wise Man's Poem

Never hide your angriness
Or cover up your tears
But tell a friend you're feeling cross or sad
Cos friends are great to talk to
When your head is blowing up
And friends can help to stop you going mad

Keep your lips in practice
When you snuggle up with love
And have a hug each time you go to town
Cos every time you kiss someone
You top them up with Life
And when you don't they keep on running down

Laugh at any time you like
And giggle when you please
And let yourself be tickled without fuss
Cos when we laugh we tell the world
It's great to be alive
Which makes the world be friendly back to us

by Purple
Ronnie

The Ways Boys and Girls Think

BOYS

Boys' brains are like great big meat pies with lots of jelly and gristle inside and their heads are made of cement

chewy fat and gristly bits

thick crust

rock hard

This means it is difficult to get new thoughts into a boy's head

let's go to the seaside
why don't we have a romantic walk?
I want to go shopping
Who wants to go to the fun fair?
can we go to the disco?

I know let's get pissed and watch football

GIRLS

Girls' brains are more like huge fluffy clouds. Sometimes this means that incredibly complicated thoughts can shoot around in them like lightning...

If Purple and Gordon are friends and Neville fancies Shirlee and Purple loves Maisy but Gordon is Shirlee's best mate then that means Gordon definitely fancies ME!

a poem about
Perfect Girls

You may think I'm being soft-headed

You may think I'm being a fool

But I would call any girl perfect

Who tells me I'm sexy and cool

How to Spot a Perfect Girl

Looks

Ideally a Perfect Girl's body is neither too fat

...nor too thin

But really, a Perfect Girl's body is fantastic if <u>she</u> likes it, whatever it looks like

see what I mean?

Clothes

What Do Perfect Girls Do?

Work

Perfect Girls have jobs that give you lots of free holidays

Hobbies

Perfect Girls think that your hobbies are very interesting and great fun

Interests

A Perfect Girl is interested in equal rights for everyone

a poem about ↓

Loving You

coo coo

How many ways do I love you?

I think there are probably two

The rumpety pump way

Is all very well

wiggle wiggle

But I like the soppy way too

s...l...o...w...

m...o...t...i...o...n

Soft focus

by Purple Ronnie

The Differences Between Boys and Girls

Girls KISS eachother's cheeks

Boys SHAKE eachother's hands

Girls LAUGH at jokes

Boys SLAP their thighs

Girls GIVE little creatures warm milk

Boys STAMP on little creatures

When girls are sad they give eachother HUGS

When boys are Sad they PUNCH eachother's chests

When girls say good bye they PAT eachother

When boys say good bye they HIT eachother on the back

GIRLS KISS, LAUGH, HUG, GIVE, AND PAT
BOYS SHAKE, SLAP, STAMP, PUNCH, AND HIT

The reason why boys do these things is that they want girls to think they are <u>hard</u>, and if you poke boys and girls in the chest you will see that boys <u>are</u> harder

But on the inside boys are very soft because when they're not with girls they spend most of their time cuddling eachother . . .

a poem about

Men

wriggle
man with
bags of
energy
wriggle

Some men I know
Make love into an art
And always keep going
Till morning
But others I know
Just roll over and fart
When they've finished the job
Then start Snoring

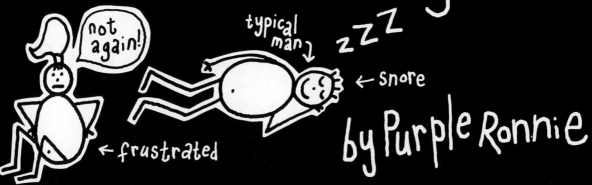

not again!

typical man
zzZ
← snore

← frustrated

by Purple Ronnie

a poem about **bestest friends** →

My Lover

I'd like to tell you something

I hope it won't offend

But if you weren't my lover

You'd be my bestest friend

us wearing saucy undies →

by Purple Ronnie

How to Write a Brilliant Love Poem

Writing Love Poems is great because you can sit down all by yourself and tell someone exactly how you feel about them without having to say it out loud and getting your feelings tangled and all your words jumbled up

LOVE INK

compare these 2 poems

Crikey I love you to pieces
My heart wants to jump up and shout
Let's walk through the flowers
And huggle for hours
And let all our loveliness out

Love Poem 1

Most people would prefer to be sent **Love Poem 1**. This is because in **Love Poem 2** I have broken all the rules. You must stick to the rules when you write Love poems or people will not love you for very long

The Rules

<u>DO</u> <u>NOT</u> tell someone they've got huge bits (unless he's a man)

<u>DO</u> use soppy words

<u>DO</u> <u>NOT</u> tell someone you're desperate to DO IT

<u>DO</u> tell them they're smashing to be with

<u>DO</u> <u>NOT</u> tell someone you DO IT with lots of other people

<u>DO</u> talk about cuddly feelings

<u>DO</u> <u>NOT</u> talk about girls' pants

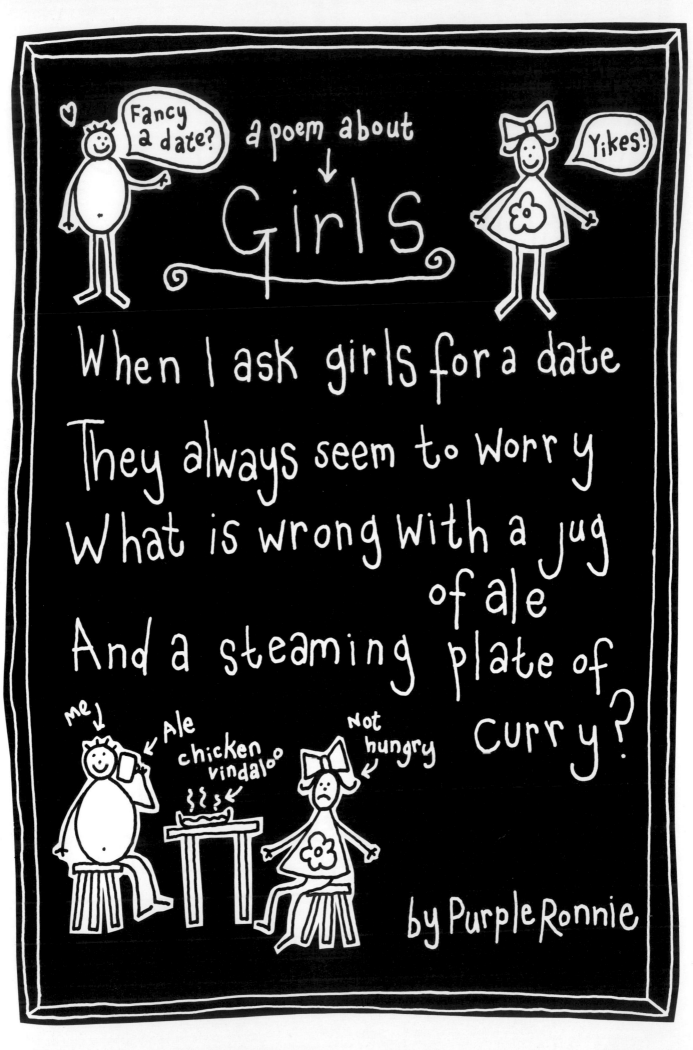

a poem about
Smiley Inside

Love makes you feel all cuddly
and warm
Love makes your tongue get all
tied
It makes you go wobbly
And weak at the knees
And all sort of smiley inside

by
purple
Ronnie

Hugging

Ever since people were invented they have spent most of their time thinking up all sorts of brainy words so they can talk to eachother about incredibly grown-up things and tell eachother how amazingly clever they are

we'll have to scrunge the wibblesnack with a tickling hose and scragglepoop the bottyhiss with a double grundle

it's either that or a full dingleslip to the trouserpipe

24 hour Dingle-slip Job 20p

The problem with words is that they are useless when you want to tell people how you're feeling and talk about what's going on INSIDE YOU

x-ray machine

a poem about

My Own Little Way

I sometimes get rather embarrassed
And don't always know what to say
When it comes to expressing my feelings
But I try in my own little way

I sort of...well... it's just that... well

shuffle shuffle

THE ONLY LANGUAGE PEOPLE CAN REALLY USE TO SAY
IMPORTANT THINGS IS THE LANGUAGE OF HUGGING

hug
master →

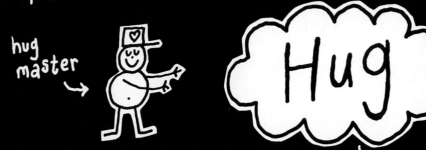

A hug is the deepest way there
is for one person to say something
to another. It is given standing
very still with the eyes closed.
You hold eachother so tightly that
your feelings are squodged together into one ginormous
feeling of L O V E L I N E S S

A cuddle is shared between 2 people who want to
say the same thing to eachother.
You can cuddle while:

sitting   or   lying down

jiggle   jiggle

you hold eachother
more loosely than
in a hug, and
jiggle around
until your feelings
are nicely shaken
about and mixed
together

YOU ALWAYS COME OUT OF A CUDDLE SMILING

Snuggle

A snuggle is used mainly for warmth and comfort and can ONLY be had lying down

snuggling is done under warm blankets or in little hidey holes

It is wet nosed and gentle and is good at keeping MONSTERS away

 yikes!

Huggle

yipee!

huggle crazy

A huggle is only used by people who are bubbling over with happiness. You can huggle while dancing, jumping, or skipping down the street. Huggles can say ANYTHING YOU LIKE. You can give crazy huggles and you can even huggle yourself!

a lovely Hugging Poem

I want you to know
That I think you are great
And although I'm a bit of a mug
If you ever need me
I'll always be near
To come round and give you
a hug

by Purple Ronnie

a poem about a
↓
Perfect Man

Most girls want a man who is perfect

But maybe not many exist

Who've got charm and panache

Several sackloads of cash

And a willy the size of your wrist

How to Spot a Perfect Man

Body

A Perfect Man's body would win any competition even though he would never dream of entering one

The Perfect Man has a **gorgeous** smile that lights up in his eyes every time he sees you

Clothes:-

Perfect Men are not half as interested in buying clothes for themselves as they are in buying clothes for you

Perfect Men never complain when you borrow their clothes

Perfect Men and Romance

The Perfect Man loves to tell you how beautiful you look - even first thing in the morning

Perfect Men always find a reason to take you out for a romantic evening

When it comes to Doing It :-

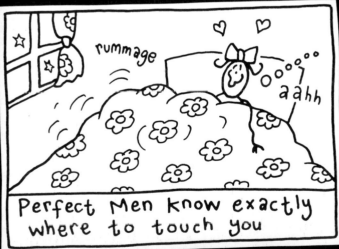

Special Tip:-
Perfect Men always cuddle you until you fall asleep

The differences between Hunks and Weeds

Boyfriends come in 2 styles:-

HUNKS: who are macho and bossy and tell you what to do all the time

AND

WEEDS: who are dreamy and funny and don't even know what to do themselves

Here is how to tell the difference:-

Girls think hunks are tough

Weeds think girls are tough

Hunks make a rumpus

Weeds make a fuss

... more differences

Hunks chew lumps of meat

Weeds cook fancy dishes

Hunks ride motorbikes

Weeds write poems

Hunks think love is rubbish

Weeds think love is an art

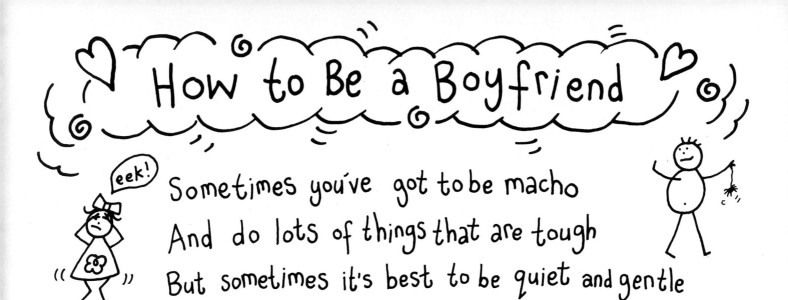

How to Be a Boyfriend

Sometimes you've got to be macho
And do lots of things that are tough
But sometimes it's best to be quiet and gentle
And say loads of soppy type stuff

It's good to have hundreds of muscles
And girls always like a nice bum
But you mustn't be hairy or sweaty
                              or fat
Or have any flab on your tum

Don't ever talk about football
Or make nasty smells in the bed
Or joke about bosoms with mates
                              in the pub
Or drink till you're out of your head

You've got to be funny and clever
And do loads of things by surprise
Like shouting out loud in the back
                    of the bus
"My girlfriend's got beautiful eyes!"

You   don't need to have too much money
But make sure you've just got enough
To buy loads of presents and chocolates
                    and flowers
And sexy silk undies and stuff

Say to your girlfriend "you're gorgeous
Your body's a twelve out of ten
You're sexy and beautiful, clever and kind"
Then tell her all over again

a poem to say

I Love You

When I am lying alone in my bed

All sorts of thoughts come into my head

Like why do I Love You as much as I do?

Then I know it's because you are You

by Purple
Ronnie

a poem about ↓

Snuggle Pie

You to me are everything

That money just can't buy

Like creamy cuddle custard

And scrumptious snuggle pie

custard love →

by Purple Ronnie

Drinking is one of the main things that keeps us alive. If we didn't drink we'd go all dry and crumbly like biscuits and people would have to sweep us up off the floor.

The main drink is water which you can tell by 3 things

1 | It's completely see-through

2 | Well...um...it's sort of ..quite...kind of... just wet | It doesn't taste of anything

3 | ? | You don't feel any nicer after you've had some

Because water is so boring lots of people got together and tried millions of experiments to invent other sorts of drinks

Some people took off their shoes and stamped on huge piles of grapes

squish
hic

Some people tried to make tasty recipes with plants and flowers

And some people just squeezed out their mouldy vegetables

whiff

The one thing they all came up with was BOOZE

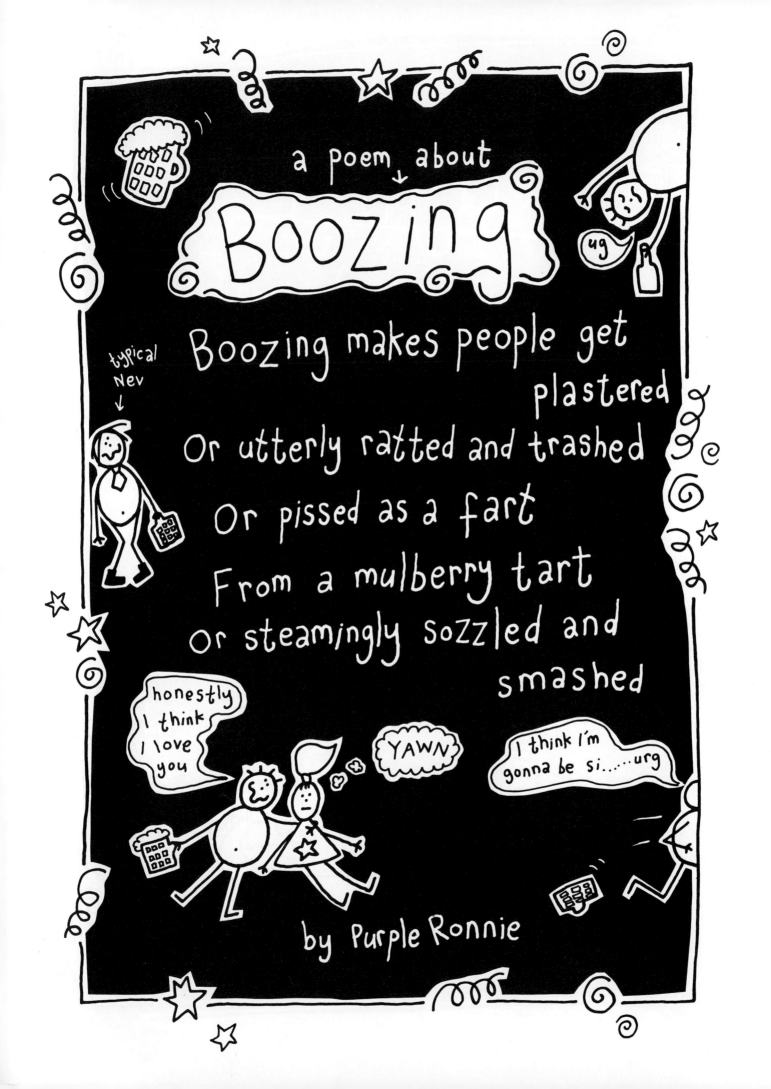

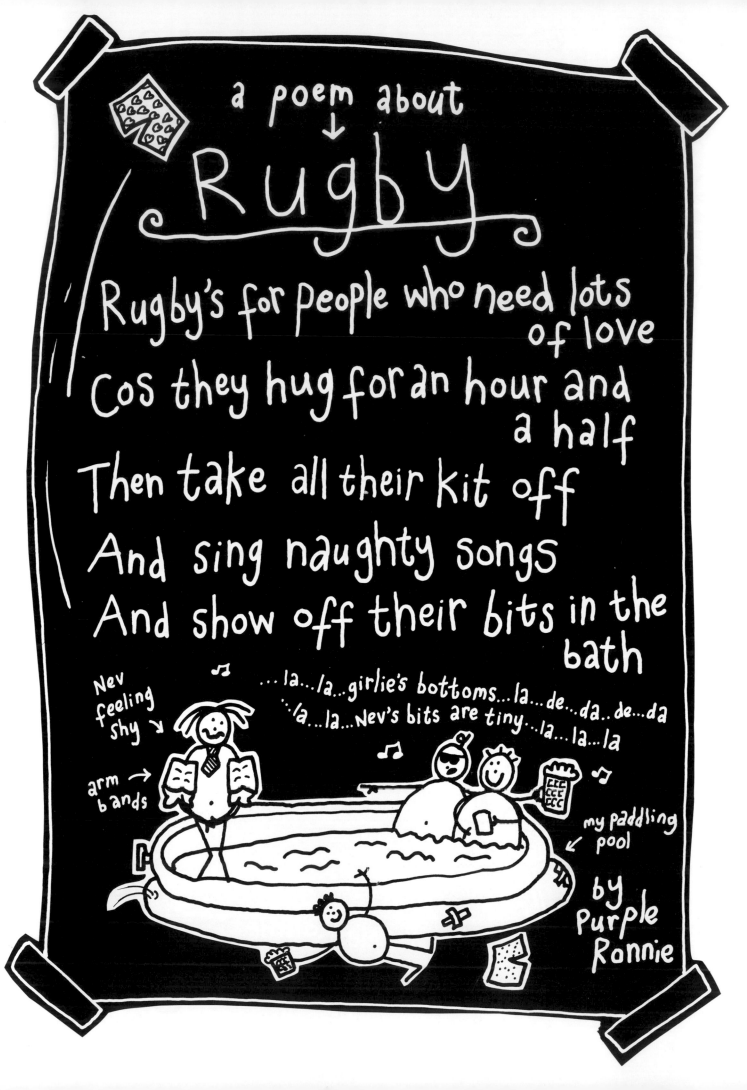

CUDDLING MATCHES

At Cuddling Matches all the men dress up in shorts and get into two gangs

There is one man who skips and dances and puts his hands up.
He is the Snuggle Judge who is called the referee

phreep

When he blows his whistle the gangs run towards him and get ready to have a mass Snuggle. They do this by bending over and holding onto each other's pants

squidge   grunt   oof

Someone tries to put a ball into the snuggle but the men are having such a cosy time that they just scrape it out of the way

The players then take it in turns to run around and make eachother fall over by hugging their legs

Some of the men in cuddling matches put special shields in their mouths in case people from the other gang try to snog them, which is **not** in the rules

me wearing my snog shield →

Rules
No Snogging

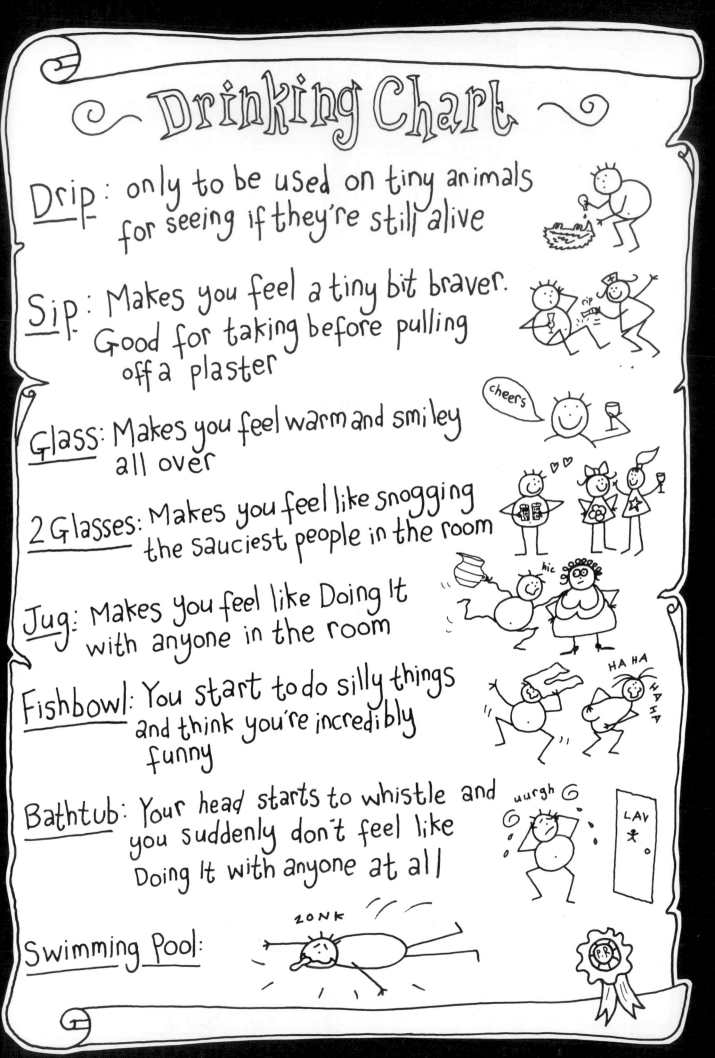

Purple Slammer

So strong it comes in teeny glasses and you can only have one sip before exploding

Fancy Fruity Cocktail

Makes you nice and healthy. There is no booze in it

Isle of Gordon Special Malt

Secret recipe known only to the MacGordons. Takes ages to make, but incredibly scrumptious. Great to drink when nattering with old friends by the fireside

Veuve de Purple Vintage Fizz

Costs loads of money. Only for special treats or when you're desperate to snog someone. Makes you fizz all over with happiness

Getting Married

Getting married is one of the most important things you can ever do. This is what happens:

First the boy asks the girl's Dad if *he* will let him marry her. This is meant to be a surprise but the girl's Mum has normally found out first

um...can I...er...do you mind...um

Doze snore

I think I'll wear my green hat...and my orange dress...and my mauve shoes

when we were your age blah blah snogging in the bushes blah blah

?

tee hee

The Dad always says yes — specially if the boy has got lots of money. Then he shakes his hand and tells hundreds of rude stories about him and the Mum

Then the Mum and the girl go shopping for millions of new clothes. They get fancy hairstyles and the girl buys a dress that is much too long for her

frizz machine

Eugene's dog

sniff sniff

Eugene

NEW HAT

KNICKERS

POINTY SHOES

BIG WHITE DRESS

PANTS

Just before the boy gets married his mates go out with him for a feast and they drink masses of beer and try to trick him into DOING IT WITH other ladies

On the day you get married you have to stand up in front of all the people in the church and the vicar asks you some questions to see how much you Love the other person

Then you must both make some promises of love which go like this

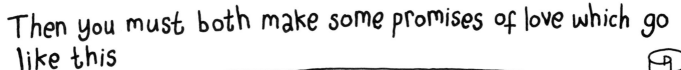

⟊⟊ L O V E   P R O M I S E S ⟊⟊

1. I promise this person that I will look after them forever, specially if they get very poorly.

2. I promise this person that I will not have rude thoughts about anyone else and that I will only ever DO IT with them <u>ever</u>.

3. I promise this person that I will share out all my private things like secrets, money and sweets.

4. I promise I won't get cross or giggle if this person whiffs in bed or goes to the lav infront of me because I love all the things about this person (even if they are horrid)

true love   sign here ↓
....

When the girl comes out of church she throws her flowers up in the air and the first person to catch them will be the next to get married

After the marriage everyone goes to a huge party with Love Pie and Cuddle cake and such a saucy drinking potion that they all dance and kiss and happy around until the whole place is bursting full of Love

Right at the end, the marrieds drive off to a secret place with all their presents where they go to bed and get ready to love eachother for the whole of the rest of their life

Old People

Old people are what you get when the most grown-up grown-ups stop trying to pretend they're young anymore. This means they can be as utterly barmy and loopy-headed as they like and everyone thinks they're incredible

The main thing old people do is gang together in clubs and go on thousands of outings

Old People Clubs

The Always Being in the Post Office Club

The Saturday morning club for selling cakes to all your friends

Differences Between Grown-ups & Old People

Grown-ups like storing money

Old People like giving money away

Grown-ups hate treats

Old People love treats

Grown-ups like fancy clothes

Old people like woolly clothes

Grown-ups like big animals

Old People like titchy animals

Grown-ups like cold drinks

old pepple like a hot cup of tea

Grown-ups are always in a hurry

old people don't care about hurrying

HEAVEN

When old people have had enough of living their Life flies out of them and whizzes up to Heaven

You can only get into Heaven if you have been good so there is quite a difficult test you have to do before you can go in

If you pass the test someone at the door gives you a ticket and it's just like a big Party where everyone floats around hugging and kissing and saying nice things to eachother

hey I really dig your hairstyle

God

The King of Heaven is called God and he's a very nice man. God is incredibly old and if you see him you must be polite and not tug his beard

er... hello your smashing majesty of wonderfulness

tug

God can see everything so do not biff or poke people when you think he's not looking

I can see you

God

Squodge

Don't try to hide
When you go to the Loo
Cos God will see
And he's bigger than you

by Purple
Ronnie

W.C

Heaven

Heaven's like a Funfair
Where all the rides are free
The clouds turn into bumper cars
And there's a hot dog tree

Everyone from history
Is floating round up there
Wearing girlie dresses
And flowers in their hair

God's in charge of parties
And his son brews up the wine
So all the folk can muck around
And have a splendid time

It is no use fibbing about what you have done because God's mates are the judges and they are <u>very</u> clever

☆

But if you have been friendly and given all your sweets to old ladies and helped poorly animals then you can go whizzing up to Heaven and have a smashing time for ever and ever

Special Tip ☆

If you have got any money left when you have your chat with God you will not be allowed into Heaven so it's best to spend it all first

The End of the World

I hope that I'm there at the End of the World
When everyone stands in a queue
And says all the wickedest things that they've done
And the bad things they've wanted to do

Naughty folk's heads will cave in and explode
And goo will spurt out of their brains
Their tummies will tangle and turn inside out
And their bottoms will burst into flames

But people like me who've been lovely and kind
Will rocket straight up to the sky
And watch the whole rumpus from big squashy beds
With loads of free ale and fudge pie

And angels will cuddle and stroke us
And say how fantastic we are
And how out of all of the people they've met
We're the smashingly coolest by far